_..unted

Edna O'Brien was born in County Clare, educated by the Sisters of Mercy in Galway and graduated as a pharmacist before going on to write her first controversial novel, *The Country Girls*, in 1960. Since then she has written over twenty-five books, including *Wild Decembers*, *In the Forest*, a biography of James Joyce and most recently, *Byron in Love*. Her plays include *A Pagan Place* (Royal Court, London), *Virginia* (on the life and writings of Virginia Woolf, Haymarket, London), *Iphigenia* (Crucible, Sheffield), *Our Father* (Almeida, London), *Family Butchers* (Magic Theatre, San Francisco) and *Triptych* (Southwark Playhouse, London). Awards include *Yorkshire Post*, *Los Angeles Times*, Writers' Guild of Great Britain, Irish PEN, the European Prize for Literature, Ulysses Medal from University College Dublin and the American National Arts Gold Medal.

EDNA O'BRIEN

Haunted

ff

faber and faber

First published in 2010
by Faber and Faber Limited
74–77 Great Russell Street
London WC1B 3DA

Typeset by Country Setting, Kingsdown, Kent CT14 8ES
Printed in England by CPI Bookmarque, Croydon, Surrey

A CIP record for this book
is available from the British Library

ISBN 978-0-571-26489-6

2 4 6 8 10 9 7 5 3 1

Haunted was first presented at the Royal Exchange Theatre, Manchester, in May 2009 and transferred to the Gaiety Theatre, Dublin, in February 2010, before a UK tour produced by Duncan C. Weldon, Paul Elliot and Lane Productions. The cast was as follows:

Mr Berry Niall Buggy
Mrs Berry Brenda Blethyn
Hazel Beth Cooke

Director Braham Murray
Designer Simon Higlett
Lighting Johanna Town
Sound Pete Rice

Introduction

Writing a play is a quite different experience to writing a novel, not harder, not easier, just different. Usually what comes first with a novel are the opening lines, these being the trigger for the necessary intensity in which one has to live for an uncharted number of years. With my plays the approach is different. I imagine a place wherein my characters get born, and with *Haunted* I first conceived of a room not in the hub of the metropolis of London, but on the outskirts, on the fringes, that physical metier reflecting the life and the aspirations of the three characters.

I have always been interested in outsiders. They are yearners, their dreaming the conveyance to 'the topless towers of Ilium'. The theatre for me conjures up magic. I am not an enthusiast of what is currently called 'committed' theatre, plays that have a supposed and immediate relevance to world events and therefore claim political precedence. It is not that I don't think that wars, famines, mass displacements are not great and profound themes, they are, but they must originate from the inside, from those living in the pith of those hells, which is why enlightened reportage often surpasses works of contemporary drama and fiction. Euripides took us to wars but charted the feelings, the ambitions, the ruthlessness and the pathos of those who went there.

In an essay on literature, Vladimir Nabokov says there are three points from which we may judge a writer, as storyteller, teacher or enchanter, but that it is the enchanter that makes for greatness. My first theatrical banquets were humble, but enchanting. Twice a year to the village where I grew up in the west of Ireland, travelling players came to exalt our humdrum lives with cloak-and-dagger dramas, where even the most censorious were carried away in that small packed hall, with six paraffin hand lamps at the front of the stage serving as footlights and men and women in gorgeous, gaudy apparel, spouting lines that were in no way relevant to ploughed fields, cattle fairs and souring marriages. I fell in love with theatre, then. I was fascinated with the alchemy by which actors and actresses could transpose themselves and carry us beyond the boundaries of our little existences to feel more than we ever knew we could. Then I came to London and saw the works of Shakespeare, Chekhov, Ibsen, Strindberg, O'Neill and Beckett flawlessly done and it was both a collective and a subjective experience. I saw how theatre both represented reality and in another way heightened it – a king looking in a mirror to see his exalted or fallen state, Winnie in *Happy Days* gabbling away to evade the quotidian.

Each unhappy family is unhappy in a different way, as Tolstoy reminds us. He could have added that the unhappy family provides a richer seam for conflict and the unexpected. Dramas of the family are a microcosm of the world at large, a cauldron in which love, hate, loyalty, suspicion, tenderness and knavery find their full and glorious expression. Settling none too blissfully in outer suburbia, I became fascinated by the hidden lives of those in the forgotten streets, an outward façade of apparent normality, but surely not without many machinations and pipe dreams behind drawn curtains. I met men and women who seemed to me the archetypes for those whom Thoreau described as living in 'quiet desperation'. I wrote a series of television plays about that world, one charting the droll odyssey of a Mr and Mrs Berry. Almost fifty years later I came to write *Haunted*, wishing to dig deeper into the lives of such characters, masking and unmasking, contriving their different dances against an gnawing loneliness. And love, binding them together and setting them apart. The theme of love is perennial, but as Eugene O'Neill said, the mystery of personality is what makes love so impossible and makes lovers at one level strangers to one another. Love is the labyrinth in which a husband and wife arrive at the cliff edge, when an enchantress such as Hazel enters as unwitting catalyst, three people trapped in a universe of emotional hunger, colliding dreams, stealth and betrayal, a locus wherein 'lies madness'.

Edna O'Brien, March 2009

HAUNTED

For Brenda, Buggy, Beth, Braham –
the stalwarts

SCENE ONE

A room in Blackheath, London.
A real wall of glass with image of tall green plants.
Two straight chairs and one rocking chair. A china
sleeping doll on a shelf.
Door to street. Second door to bedroom.
A bamboo screen to kitchen area.
Three figures on stage in dim light.
Mr Berry in faded maroon velvet jacket, downstage.
Mrs Berry in hat and coat standing near entrance to
bedroom.
Hazel in frayed cream-lace wedding dress, by door to
street.

Mr Berry Stay . . . stay.

Mrs Berry (*abjuring*) Stay? Stay?

Hazel (*frightened*) Let go of me.

Darkness.
Lights come up.
On a side table, volumes of Shakespeare and Mr
Berry's tortoiseshell spectacles.
Mr Berry (Jack, aged about sixty), in sweater and
carpet slippers sets down an aluminium water can
filled with water, then hangs the secateurs on a nail on
the wall. Beside it is a straw panama hat with purple
ribbon. His voice is refined, educated and varies in
pitch, depending on whether he is talking to the
audience or to the two other characters.
Door to street creaks slowly back and forth.
Mrs Berry's voice emanates from the dark as she
enters from bedroom in her white factory overall, her

3

hair dyed strawberry blonde, high winged arc above the crown, covered in a very fine, almost invisible hairnet, blood-red nails, blood-red lipstick. She is in her fifties. Her voice aspires to being grand but at times she slips.

Mrs Berry There's a kink in you, Mr Berry . . . an unclean spirit.

She walks around him slowly, expecting a reply, gets none and exits from where she came.
Hazel, in her twenties, in wedding dress, enters from street door, crosses in front of him, reciting in a winning whisper.

Hazel
'The red rose whispers of passion
And the white rose breathes of love.
O, the red rose is a falcon
And the white rose is a dove.'

She goes.

Mr Berry (*more alert*) Not a kink, Gladys . . . enchantment . . . enchanted . . . the precipice. What did the poet say? (*Thinks.*) 'Twice or thrice have I known thee, before I knew thy face or name.' Like a bloodhound my wife, Gladys, sniffed danger from the outset . . . sang dumb . . . in marriage all is perceived . . . though much withheld . . . Infinite, the book of secrets . . . (*Briskly.*) Never knew her age . . . never knew whether she was older or younger than me . . . hid her passport . . . never clapped eyes on it. Even when we travelled . . . she'd hold it up, the page already open for the official to stamp, then she'd snap it shut . . . and give me one of her 'mind your own business, Mr Berry' looks. I named a rosebush after her – the blush rose from China . . . sturdy . . . no scent . . . remarkable thorns. (*Reflective.*) To be again in Lismore . . . I would find dog roses for dear Mother in the woods around

4

home . . . place them on her pillow . . . dinner guests downstairs . . . Tom the old retainer with dropsy – (*he mimes it*) spilling the gravy . . . Saddle of hare and diplomat pudding – keeping up appearances. Turned my back on the place after I crossed the water . . . other interests . . . mostly of a carnal nature . . . no shortage of girls . . . there for the asking. I brought Gladys home for the honeymoon . . . dreadful, dreadful . . . she didn't fit in . . . *persona non grata* at Glebe House . . . 'Crikey, what's this?' she said, sucking the stalk of the asparagus. A yeowoman . . . that's what Mother called her . . . kept getting her name wrong . . . called her Mabel after the maid we had . . . at each other's throats . . . female fangs. Never saw the place again. In other hands now . . . a foreigner . . . Dutch. Had the post of clerk at Epsom racecourse . . . making sure everything was in good order. God the excitement before a race, the adrenalin, the colours . . . the jockeys' colours and the ladies in their pink and peach . . . big money . . . big betting . . . trainers on edge down at the paddock . . . the horses ditto . . . big money and fornication . . . opportunities . . . hotel suites . . . devilment . . . *la chasse* . . . (*Confiding.*) I was a married man, yet I fell. She was called Greta, from a racing dynasty. I always fell. Years before, I fell for Gladys and swore – (*searches*) constancy. It was in The Catherine Wheel . . . lovely old-fashioned pub, ornate gold lettering on the black coping . . . 'Select Wines and Ports' . . . Gladys hauling the crates of beer . . . gave me the eye . . . gave all and sundry the eye . . . Half a year before things transpired . . . in the shed . . . on the beer barrels . . . the strength in her, the way she lay back and received me . . . more versatile than I, by far. 'Go for your life, Lady Carruthers' – that's what she named our mischiefs. The strength in her, and the appetite . . . the appetite for life. She usen't to talk much then . . . different afterwards . . . tongue always wagging . . . a mile a minute . . . such notions . . . (*Humorous.*) Mad for royalty . . . Bourbons, Romanoffs, Windsors, any old royalty . . . all the same to her . . . the bedroom modest by any standard . . . named Versailles . . . ongoing regret concerning the absence of a staircase, dreamed of making an entrance. Poor Gladys. Nearly strangled her that bitter time, during the Greta interlude. In my sleep . . . in her sleep . . . in both our sleeps . . . wakened with my hand around her neck . . . her head off the pillow . . . banging her up and down . . . no voice left in her . . . turned on the lamp . . . terror in her eyes . . . stark naked terror.

Hazel walks behind the glass panel and Mr Berry sees her image as she crosses.

Hazel! Her waist, her hourglass waist, corsage of violets pinned to her lapel . . . a changeling.

Hazel has gone from view and there is a knock on the street door.

'I've come about the garment.' Those were her very words.

He opens the door.
    Hazel in a tweed jacket with a corsage of violets in her lapel, long black skirt and black beret which covers her hair completely.

Hazel I've come about the garment.

Mr Berry (*over-courteous*) Welcome. *Willkommen. Bienvenue. Enchanté.*

Hazel If it's inconvenient . . . I can come back another time.

Mr Berry Not at all . . . not in the least . . . it's perfectly delightful . . . come inside.

Hazel enters. She is painfully shy. Though in her twenties, she seems and behaves much younger.

Mr Berry Won't you sit?

Hazel I'll just look at the coatee.

Mr Berry smiles to cover up his bafflement.

(*Apologetic.*) It's for a client . . . she's been invited to a black-and-gold ball . . . and the theme is the twenties.

Mr Berry The roaring twenties.

Hazel The dealer in Greenwich didn't have one, she sent me to a thrift shop near here, the Primavera, and a woman looked up a book and sent me to this address.

Mr Berry (*to audience*) I twigged. Gladys sold clothes that she'd grown out of, down at Primavera . . . the money was for the holiday . . . Agadir . . . kept in a jug . . . coins and notes . . . (*To Hazel.*) You've come a very long way, by bus?

Hazel Two buses and the underground.

Mr Berry Tch tch tch, and the lift isn't working . . . three flights of dirty stairs . . . they never sweep it . . . you must be expiring . . . do sit.

Hazel I won't keep you.

Mr Berry Not keeping me . . . it's a pleasure . . . if only I could show you the garden . . . if only it were June . . . a cornucopia of roses . . . or even, July . . . (*Softly.*) Sit.

Hazel sits and stares down at her folded hands in her lap.

Mr Berry We haven't met.

Hazel Hazel.

Mr Berry Berry – Quincy.

He sits.

Mr Berry You are not from these parts?

Hazel No . . . I live over Chelsea way, beyond World's End.

Mr Berry (*wooing*) Do I not detect a Celtic lilt?

Hazel Mother was Irish . . . she came here very young . . . she was in service. Later on she had her own stall . . . We travelled to fairs and carnivals . . . she read the tea leaves.

Mr Berry She had the gift?

Hazel Yes, like her grandmother.

Mr Berry And you have the gift?

Hazel (*shaking her head*) No . . . it skips a generation.

Mr Berry (*with wonder*) You travelled all over, to fairs and carnivals. A gypsy, Hazel.

Hazel We didn't mix.

Mr Berry You speak so beautifully. You strike me as an actress.

Hazel I'd have stage fright.

Mr Berry But your enunciation is . . . impeccable.

Hazel (*somewhat abashed*) I teach elocution, in a convent in Roehampton . . . do my stall Fridays and Saturdays, mostly lace.

Mr Berry How . . . edifying. I used to go to the theatre a lot . . . in my younger days. (*Warming to his subject.*) I saw a very engrossing play . . . most compelling . . . a man on a bench in Central Park in New York, having a bit of a ponder, when another man comes along, sits down next to him, and they enter into an altercation . . . Things got quite heated, quite nasty, some mention of a dog.

Hazel That's *Zoo Story*.

Mr Berry Exactly . . . *Zoo Story* . . . I expect you're very *au fait*.

Hazel Sometimes parents ask me to take the children. Matinees.

Mr Berry Lucky them. You teach them the Bard?

Hazel No . . . it's more elementary . . . the vowels and the consonants . . . 'vanna manna' . . . 'famma namma' . . . 'Billie Button bit a buttered bun' . . . (*Gets carried away.*) 'The teeth and the lips and the tip of the tongue . . . tra la la la la la . . .'

> 'Up the airy mountain and down the rushy glen
> We daren't go a-hunting for fear of little men,
> Wee folk, good folk, trooping all together,
> Green jacket, red cap and grey cock's feather!'

She stops suddenly, overcome with embarrassment.

Mr Berry Could I offer you something, a drop of Madeira, warm your cockles?

Hazel I won't, thank you.

Mr Berry takes the open book of Shakespeare off the table.

Mr Berry I like the Bard . . . (*Intimate voice.*) He keeps me company . . . (*Pointing to the volumes.*) I got those for a song at one of the markets . . . I might have encountered you, in your stall . . . in your bowers of lace.

Hazel It's not as lovely as in Mother's time . . . she had exquisite pieces, embroidered with sprigs and sprays and shamrocks . . . from Antwerp, Chantilly, Burano, Flanders, Carrickmacross – veils, lappets, handkerchiefs, fans, berthas, parasols.

Mr Berry Excuse me, Hazel, but what is a bertha?

Hazel (*describing it with her hands*) It's a wide collar that hangs around the neck and extends down onto the – (*hesitant*) chest.

Mr Berry I see.

Hazel We had books that we used to read up . . . what such and such an Empress chose for her trousseau . . . her bed, her valance, her lying-in bed. (*Lively.*) And there was this manual called *Voyaging to Marry Land*. (*Saddish.*) We had a plan to visit the lace countries.

Mr Berry You lost her?

Hazel I did.

Mr Berry I know how you feel.

Hazel I can't get used to it . . . I still think she'll come back, in fact she does come back in my sleep, in my dreams . . . she stands by my bed.

Mr Berry (*his voice half breaking*) Ever since my wife . . . (*He turns away.*) I feel the toll of Father Time . . . abysms of it . . . I see Cassidy, an old chum . . . we meet equidistant between Epsom and here for our moratoriums . . . barely throw two words to one another, but it's company. (*Rallying.*) In the summer I'm rarely indoors, pottering in the garden. Had it been summer I would not have heard you. I would have missed you . . . It's lacklustre at the moment . . . still, spring is a-coming . . . What is it about spring and the daffodils? (*Going closer to her.*) I know you know it. It's on the tip of your tongue.

Hazel It . . . isn't.

Mr Berry (*encouraging her*)
　　　　　　　　　　　'Daffodils
　That come before the swallow dares, and take
　The winds of March with beauty, violets dim . . .'
Help me, Hazel, help me.

Hazel
'. . . Violets dim,
   But sweeter than the lids of Juno's eyes
   Or Cytherea's breath; pale primroses
   That die unmarried, ere they can behold
   Bright Phoebus in his strength – a malady
   Most incident to maids . . .'

She stops abruptly.

Mr Berry My my, how wondrous. I feel quite transported.
I can see you on the stage – Ophelia . . . with her garlands
of flowers . . . in the brook . . . aslant the willows . . .
hoar frost on her gown . . . (*Decisive.*) You're wasted on
young children.

Hazel I see some adults.

Mr Berry In World's End?

Hazel No . . . one lady in Wimpole Street who hopes to
make a comeback and a Duke who lives in The Savoy.

Mr Berry Lives in The Savoy!

Hazel He's a recluse.

Mr Berry And does he recite 'Billy Button bit a buttered
bun'?

Hazel He has a stammer.

Mr Berry (*excited*) I read an interesting thing concerning
a French actor who stammered, yet the moment he trod
those boards, all was fluent. The same with your recluse
perhaps.

Hazel No . . . he prefers reading and then we discuss it . . .
At the moment it's *Othello*. Why he allowed himself to
be driven to such mad jealousies.

Mr Berry (*curious*) I am assuming the Duke has reason
to be jealous.

Hazel We don't discuss personal matters.

Mr Berry (*resuming his grief*) My dear wife . . . I planted a rosebush for her . . . the red rose . . . 'old blush' it was called . . . sturdy . . . remarkable thorns. (*More authoritative.*) There is a common misapprehension that roses are English but they are not. They originated in the East and were brought to Greece and Crete and hence to these shores . . . The ramonas . . . the ramblers . . . the damask – (*With wonder.*) The scent of the damask. Did you know that the tears of Mary Magdalene bleached the red rose white and according to another tradition the rose is linked to the nightingale who lets out a protesting cry whenever a rose is plucked. The symbol of the rose is silence . . . hence *sub rosa*.

Hazel You know a lot.

Mr Berry They write these little homilies on the seed packet. Yes, creaks, emptiness, abysms of time, a time to weep and a time to laugh, a time to mourn and – (*almost inaudible*) a time to resurrect.

> *Pause.*
> *Hazel coughs nervously, the cue that she must go.*

Mr Berry (*briskly*) The coatee, the coatee.

> *Mr Berry rushes to the inner room.*
> *Hazel searches in her tiny purse for her money, takes it out and holds it in her fist.*
> *Mr Berry returns with a blue angora cardigan with white trimming, already speaking.*

Mr Berry The thing is I can't lay my hands on it . . . I'll have found it by next week . . . I do recall it . . . old gold . . . like chain mail . . . Look, why don't you try this? Try it on at home . . . you might find some use for it . . . with your dresses or your slacks . . . mix-and-match, I believe that's the vernacular nowadays.

Hazel I couldn't.

Mr Berry You could if I asked you . . . if I pleaded . . . if I said you would make an old man very happy by accepting.

Hazel How much is it?

Mr Berry Nonsense . . . people like you and I are not carpetbaggers . . . we are not Shylocks . . . we are 'Friends, Romans, countrymen, lend me your ears.' (*Confidential voice.*) I'll let you in on a little secret . . . I have sometimes thought I might join some amateur company, chance my arm. Modest parts . . . that servant – (*thinking*) Firs, that gets forgotten, locked in a cupboard. You see, if I could impose on you to have a few lessons it would start me off.

Hazel But you don't need me.

Mr Berry I do I do, for the music, the feeling, the inflections, the cadences . . . Shall we say, same time next week? We'll brave the Bard.

> *He hands her the cardigan and sees her out.*
> *Hazel goes.*
> *In his excitement he scarcely knows what to do; he sits on the chair where she sat, sits on the other chair, brings them closer, walks around, all the while talking.*

Mr Berry So shy . . . stricken. (*Gleeful.*) 'Billic Button bit a buttered bun' . . . Her aura . . . Jesus . . . this room will never be the same . . . the small of her waist . . . eyes . . . like gooseberries. She has to come back . . . she will want to repay me . . . I'll see her one more time or perhaps a few. Quincy, Quincy. (*Addressing himself in the wall mirror.*) 'O step between me and my madness . . .' (*Stern.*) 'Let not thy tongue speak thy thoughts.' (*Animated.*)

> 'Up the airy mountain and down the rushy glen
> We daren't go a-hunting, for fear of little men,

Wee folk, good folk, trooping altogether,
Green jacket, red cap and grey cock's feather!'

*Mrs Berry enters in a fawn coat with a floral scarf
loosely tied so as not to disturb the summit of her hair.
She has a large brown-leather handbag with knuckled
amber clasp. Hearing him talking to himself she looks
around suspiciously, sniffing.*

Mrs Berry What's got into you? There's a kink in you,
Mr Berry . . . and why are the chairs like that, who's been
here? If you saw that Greta bitch again you'd pay for it,
pay dear . . . and so would she, I'd square up to her, I'd
put a knife through her.

Mr Berry Now now, Gladys . . . no retrospect . . . she
married the trainer . . . you know she did . . . you read it
aloud to me from *The Field*.

Mrs Berry He will have left her by now . . . They report
the weddings but not the partings. (*In full spate.*) That
time you went to her, she didn't want you, did she, once
the novelty was over, didn't want your dirty linen, your
socks, your merchandise. (*More vaunting.*) Or else you
missed me, more than you thought you would. (*Sharper.*)
When I rang and said I would be dropping off your
effects and your library, she got the wind up. Here you
were, the prodigal, back in the kitchen, all meek and mild.
I walked straight past you to ready the dinner, it was
mince, for spaghetti bolognaise. (*Emphatic.*) I'd told no
one that you'd gone . . . couldn't . . . Desertion has to be
borne alone. (*Sad.*) It was like a grave here.

Mr Berry Tush. We promised we would not war.

Mrs Berry We crawled back up. I minded of course. I
shall always mind – (*dramatic*) to my very marrow.

Mr Berry (*discursive*) How was today?

Mrs Berry Same as yesterday, same as every day.

Mr Berry How's Iris?

Mrs Berry You hate her.

Mrs Berry walks behind the screen and turns, swinging the handbag and scolding.

You sluggard . . . the stove's nearly out . . . and the stew's not on.

Mr Berry It shall be . . . anon.

Mrs Berry There's no anon . . . a stew takes a minimum of two hours and then one hour to cool and skim the fat off . . . It will have to be sardines on toast . . . I was quite looking forward to a hot cassoulet after a trying day.

Mr Berry Was it trying, my pet?

Mrs Berry (*tartly*) Of course it was, it always is. Young girls, whippersnappers, all they're thinking of is their figures. On my feet, at my time of life, my corns, my veins, my blood sugar at the end of the day just dropped to nought. If I don't eat I fade . . . I fade away. (*Vexed.*) A trainee put left-hand arms on the right joints of fifty dolls . . . the whole tray had to be redone.

Mr Berry But there are left-handed people, I once read the figure and it's quite considerable, so why not have left-hand dolls?

Mrs Berry Don't be so stupid.

Mr Berry You're very invigorated . . . perturbed –

Mrs Berry (*interrupting*) What's got into you? You haven't even pared the sprouts.

Mr Berry I was . . . occupied.

Mrs Berry You don't seem to grasp it . . . the roles are reversed . . . you do the cleaning, washing, ironing and cushion plumping before noon and in the afternoon you plan our evening menu and become chef. Whilst I am the breadwinner.

Mr Berry (*placating*) So you are, my pet.

Mrs Berry (*brightening*) So I am. I've been told it on the grapevine . . . I'm to be promoted . . . I'm to be made supervisor . . . Iris will take it badly . . . me, above her, in a different category altogether, a different overall, a white overall. Ruling the roost. Poor Iris, up at twenty-five past six each morning, out of the house at five to seven to catch the seven ten. They should never have moved, much nicer to be in the heart of things, in the hub, here in Blackheath . . . Redhill is too far out, not even a suburb.

She sits in the rocking chair and puts her feet out for him to take off her shoes.

Mr Berry Something happened.

Mrs Berry What happened?

Mr Berry Something odd.

Mrs Berry Odd.

Mr Berry There was a box at the door . . . a very suspicious-looking . . . cardboard box.

Mrs Berry What was in it?

Mr Berry I don't know.

Mrs Berry There is a box at the door and you don't investigate it . . . In this day and age . . . it could be a bomb . . . a home-made bomb . . . What kind of moron are you? Did you call the police?

Mr Berry No. Because when I opened the door the second time, it wasn't there . . . it was gone.

Mrs Berry Pray, what did you do between opening the door the first time, sighting the box, and opening the door the second time? What did you do, read *Hamlet*, to be or not to be bludgeoned to death? I know what you did, you read and you tippled and you dozed . . . it's the depression, that's what it is, it's got a grip on you, no use sitting here and reading *Hamlet*, *Hamlet* will not help, read that book I got out of the library, Mr Gaylord Hauser, *Look Younger, Live Longer*. (*Reciting*.) 'Better and better in every way in every day, Caesar and Lepidus take to the hills, wiggledy woggledy woo.' No more napping and no more cat napping and no giving in to depression.

Mr Berry I've never felt more blessed in my whole life, Gladys.

Mrs Berry That is the upside of depression, the high, what you need is to strike the meridian, the happy medium, just as I do. (*Alert*.) Why did you say you've never felt more blessed in your whole life, Gladys?

Mr Berry Spring . . . the daffodils . . .

> 'Cytherea's breath; pale primroses
> That die unmarried, ere they can behold
> Bright Phoebus in his strength.'

Mrs Berry This is . . . peculiar.

Mr Berry There wasn't a box at the door.

Mrs Berry (*triumphant*) I knew there wasn't . . . I could tell, it was one of your, caprices.

Mr Berry Sit down, Gladys.

Mr Berry sits on the chair that Hazel sat on and gestures Mrs Berry to sit beside him.

It's not good.

Mrs Berry What's not good? A moment ago you were in the throes of happiness.

Mr Berry Yes, because the problem has been diagnosed in the nick of time.

Mrs Berry What?

Mr Berry The lump. (*Loud whisper.*) The growth.

Mrs Berry It's benign.

Mr Berry It's not benign any more . . . Tricky, that's what he said.

Mrs Berry tries to pull the top of his trousers to look in, but he thwarts her.

Mrs Berry Who says?

Mr Berry Cooper.

Mrs Berry He's an idiot.

Mr Berry Sinister was another word he used.

Mrs Berry I'll go there first thing tomorrow morning.

Mr Berry You can't . . . you're *persona* not gratis in that surgery since you reported them.

Mrs Berry I'll march in there . . . I'll insist on being seen. Mrs Gladys Eileen Berry, née Cuddahy.

Mr Berry I'll have to have tests . . . It's best that we keep on his right side . . . it's best you keep with Watson and I keep with Cooper . . . that way we have a better option, two old fogies like us. (*Singing.*)

'Dr Watson, Dr Cooper
Dr King and Dr Knox
Not forgetting Dr Fletcher
Who will take away the pox.'

What about a drop of Madeira before we get the dinner on? Drown our woes . . . what about it?

Mrs Berry (*almost coy*) I wouldn't mind.

> *Mr Berry goes behind the screen.*
> *Mrs Berry looks at herself in the wall mirror, sucks her cheeks in.*
> *Mr Berry returns with two water glasses filled with Madeira, hands her one.*

Mrs Berry (*coy*) It's impossible to argue with you Mr Berry, you're like quicksilver, that's your métier.

> *They drink.*

Mr Berry There has to be tests . . . They've moved one of the hospitals to Carshalton . . . cutbacks . . . government cutting back . . . (*Timid.*) I might not be able –

Mrs Berry (*cutting in*) Oh yes you are coming, you are coming to Agadir, we've paid the deposit, we are not letting it go.

Mr Berry You could take Iris . . .

Mrs Berry Fred wouldn't hear of that . . . they're inseparable . . . When she was in the hospital for the hysterectomy, he had a bed moved in next to her, he won't let her wear a vest.

Mr Berry (*curious*) Why not?

Mrs Berry (*ignoring the question*) If we can't go, then we won't go . . . Sod the deposit, sod the down payment, sod it. It's probably a false alarm . . . you've had boils and growths and carbuncles before . . . Remember? We stooped them in warm water and witch hazel . . . they come and go . . . they're like yo-yos . . . they're psychosomatic . . . One of your complexes.

Mr Berry He didn't think so.

Mrs Berry The way I looked forward to it.

Mr Berry (*humouring her*) You'll come back in a kaftan, refreshed. Maybe you'll bring me a camel rod . . . do they have camel rods in the desert?

Mrs Berry (*snappy*) Of course they have camel rods in the desert. The desert is full of camels and turbaned men in flowing garments . . . herding them with camel rods. (*Clinking his glass.*) You've got to come . . . think how I've saved and saved . . . collecting coupons . . . we didn't splash out at Christmas . . . sundry economies . . . I've been living for it . . . (*Affected accent.*) You linking me into the dining room each evening and holding my chair ere I sat down, talking to me and not reading the newspaper and not reading *Hamlet* . . . then back in our chalet, an open fire, that's what the brochure says, the evening fire already lit, a servant serving us mint tea . . . and bonbons . . . the fire flames dancing on the whitewashed walls, next to one another as of yore. (*Ribbing him.*) 'Go for your life, Lady Carruthers.'

Mr Berry Do you think there is a divinity that shapes our end?

Mrs Berry I don't want you sick . . . can't have you sick, Jack Berry . . . it would be awful to lose you . . . Loving someone . . . that's what life is about . . . a drink, a cuddle . . . You will come . . . they're bound to have a doctor in a five-star hotel.

Mr Berry I've been mulling over it ever since I got back in . . . fretting . . . I knew you'd be upset . . . and what I've decided is, we'll have a second holiday at the end of the season . . . We'll go to Ireland . . . travel round.

Mrs Berry You swore you'd never go back to Glebe House.

Mr Berry They're all dead now . . . it makes no difference. I'd like to see the old haunts, the kitchen garden . . . the lake . . . the fuchsia hedges, the mountains and the reeks.

Mrs Berry (*mellowing a little from the drink*) What was they called? The Magillacuddy Reeks . . . I swam near there . . . or rather I bathed. Not a stitch on me . . . I could kill your mother . . . cutting us out of her will . . . Still, I got the Balenciaga and the seed pearls . . . Getting my name wrong – Mabel, who wants to be called Mabel? Yes, I swam naked and you read to me, to educate me. (*Fondly.*) Then you'd put the book down, for the coaxing, calling me La Belle something without mercy, 'cause I was a tease . . . Buried in my bosom. (*Curious.*) Was it in Cork or Kerry or was that the time we rode over as far as Waterford . . . such prowess with the oars . . . A cutter you called your little skiff. (*Scolding.*) Oh, the mischief, the mischiefs . . . my girdle in a rock pool in Lismore.

Mr Berry Quite a seafarer, that little cutter.

Mrs Berry We conceived on the Black Mountain.

Mr Berry Don't, dearest.

Mrs Berry You cried as much as me, more. It was you that washed the bloodied sheet and put it away in the trunk . . . with my wedding dress. Our child.

Mr Berry goes behind the screen.

Mr Berry (*offstage*) It was all long ago.

Mrs Berry (*loudly*) It did something to us . . . we aged.

Mr Berry returns with the bottle of Madeira and glasses, sings softly as he pours.

Mr Berry
'Who in the song so sweet,
Eileen aroon!
Who in the dance so sweet,

21

Eileen aroon!
Dear were her charms to me,
Dearer her laughter free,
Dearest her constancy,
Eileen aroon!'

Mrs Berry You taught me that song, Jack.

Mr Berry So I did.

He hands her the very full glass and they drink.

Mrs Berry (*gazing up at him*) Not every couple can claim
to be as happy as us. We find each other fascinating, we
discover new things each day . . . each evening . . . none
of those long sullen silences, absolutely none. (*Raising her
glass.*) Live and grow old with me, the best is yet to be.

Lights down.

SCENE TWO

Lights come up.
   Black dress with a diamante clasp hanging on screen.
   *Hazel and Mr Berry are standing. Hazel's hair is long
and loose, dark with deep copper glints.*
   He is reading the lessons from an exercise book.

Hazel Vanna manna famma namma vanna manna
famma namma vanna manna famma namma.

Mr Berry (*enthralled*) Your hair . . . is on fire.

Hazel Vanna manna famma namma vanna manna.

Mr Berry Vanna manna manna famma damma – oh, it's
a tongue-twister, Hazel.

Hazel The teeth and the lips and the tip of the tongue,
Mr Berry.

A skunk sat on a stump and the stump thought the skunk stunk and the skunk thought the stump stunk.

Mr Berry (*leafing through the book*)
'Up the airy mountain and down the rushy glen
We daren't go a-hunting for fear of little men,
Wee folk, good folk, trooping all together.
Green jacket, red cap and grey cock's feather!'

Hazel Good, good.

Mr Berry (*unabated*)
'The fairest things have the fleetest end,
Their scent survives their close:
But the rose's scent is bitterness
To him who loves the rose.'

He puts the book down, expiring from his labours.

May I sit?

Hazel You may . . . but not for long.

She hands him a poem on a single sheet of yellow parchment.

I brought you this.

Mr Berry takes it reverently, gazes at it.

Mr Berry In your own hand.

Hazel Read it.

Mr Berry You read it.

Hazel hesitates, then recites the last three lines of the poem.

Hazel
'Remember me, in God's name; when
The grey mist rises from the swamp
And reaches the palings of the fence,
Remember me.'

Mr Berry (*overcome*) Whoever wrote that has had his wings clipped.

Hazel Alexander Blok. It says on the back of his book he died of acute melancholia.

Mr Berry (*gently*) 'The love of love and her soft hours.' (*Practical.*) A sentiment much mocked in our callow era. (*Getting carried away.*) Plato did not mock it, oh no, 'O you, Dion, who through love brought delirium into my heart.' It has been said that Plato did everything to dispel that love . . . he did not follow the young boy south to Sicily, and yet it was waiting . . . his destiny . . . There is a Turkish proverb to that effect. (*Quietly.*) Have you ever been in love, Hazel?

Pause.

Hazel Yes.

Mr Berry Ac-tor?

Hazel No.

Mr Berry Poet? Painter?

Hazel Wrong, wrong, wrong.

Mr Berry A horse trainer, a tycoon, a tax exile?

Hazel Hardly. He has an old shabby green overcoat.

Mr Berry Yet it is love, is it not?

Hazel Maybe.

Mr Berry Does the man in the shabby green overcoat live by the World's End?

Hazel No, across the water. (*Suddenly*) It was a bit like . . . coming here . . . a bit of a muddle. I was rung up and told to go and see this man . . . give him a few tips for his public speaking. He didn't want tips . . . he was

24

his own person, he knew what he wanted and straight away I knew he knew what he wanted . . . You can always see it in someone . . . they're quite remote with people because of this other thing, this burning other thing, this conviction in his eyes . . . He didn't want advice from me, so I said, 'I better be off,' and he jumped up. 'Don't go don't go,' and went and brought back a mug of tea, all milky . . . asked me what I did . . . things like that . . . they were buzzing him from another room, he was a man with no spare time and still . . . we lingered. He said a strange thing, he said that people thought he was not emotional, but he was, he simply had to keep it under lock and key. Just as I was leaving I dropped my handbag, my hairbrush, my purse, my clobber . . . all over the floor and, we knelt down to gather them up, and . . .

Mr Berry (*quickly*) He kissed you.

Hazel No.

Mr Berry But you knew.

Hazel When he was helping me into my coat, he asked if it was possible to meet again.

Mr Berry (*excited*) An assignation.

Hazel Yes, but no. At a quarter to five each evening for weeks afterwards my telephone would ring and I would pick it up and listen but nobody spoke.

Mr Berry Cold feet.

Hazel I expect so.

Mr Berry What do you think he would have said?

Hazel I don't know . . . The place, the time, or the no place, or the no time.

Mr Berry And you never saw him again.

Hazel Once, in an elevator, with his cohorts.

Mr Berry He has cohorts.

Hazel He saw me, but he looked away.

Mr Berry I should like to meet this chap, call him out into the yard and give him a good cuffing.

Hazel Why would you do that?

Mr Berry (*clasping his two arms*) To bring a Cressida to a Troilus.

Hazel Troilus has to come to Cressida of his own accord, she would not want it any other way.

Mr Berry holds the black dress on its hanger for her to admire.

I wouldn't have any wear for it.

Mr Berry You will. He will escape the cohorts one night, he will be standing outside your window, your chevalier. It's what you dream, in the wee hours.

Hazel Don't, Mr Berry.

Mr Berry Or in The Savoy, as you pass, 'The woman in black', weaving her way in and out between the tables, the flowers and the foliage, under the lit chandeliers, strangers athirst for a tress of that hair. (*Whisper.*) Do take it.

She holds the dress in front of her, clearly enamoured of it. She looks at the label.

Hazel It's French . . . it's a French model.

Mr Berry Wear it, stand by your window when the lights are quenched and he will have come in the long green overcoat, carrying a black thornstick to beat off suitors and wild dogs – yes, Hazel, all things come to she who waits.

Waltz music.
  Hazel backs away holding the dress close up to her.
  Mr Berry follows, half dancing.
  Hazel goes.
  Mr Berry dances alone.
  Lights down.

SCENE THREE

Morning.
  Mr Berry with shoe kit, polishing various pairs of his own shoes. He enjoys doing it.
  Mrs Berry calls from the inner room.

Mrs Berry (*offstage*) Can you hear me?

  Mr Berry does not reply.
  Mrs Berry comes from the inner room carrying a buckled metal coat hanger.

I say, did you see my edge-to-edge?

Mr Berry Your what?

Mrs Berry My edge-to-edge coat . . . the one I bought at the January sales the year before last, my light coat for summer evenings.

Mr Berry What colour is it?

Mrs Berry Grey.

Mr Berry You haven't got a grey coat.

Mrs Berry I have.

Mr Berry How funny, I thought it was fawn.

Mrs Berry So you remember it then.

Mr Berry You must have sent it to the cleaners.

Mrs Berry I haven't. What have you done with it?

Mrs Berry pinions him against the wall, the hook of the coat hanger digging into his forehead.

Mr Berry What are you doing, Gladys?

Mrs Berry Trying to penetrate the nooks and crannies of that serpentine mind of yours . . . to catch the conscience of the King, Mr Berry.

Mr Berry It could be anywhere . . . it could be in the factory . . . you might have left it on a bus . . . you left your umbrella on the 39A bus.

Mrs Berry I did not leave it on a bus.

Mr Berry You left your umbrella.

Mrs Berry An umbrella is a different thing, an umbrella is an accessory, a coat is an essential.

Mr Berry You paid the gas bill twice . . . It's the pills you're taking for the blood pressure . . . they're interfering with your memory . . . your marbles . . . your faculties.

He wrenches the coat hanger from her.

Mrs Berry My mind is perfectly lucid . . . the aberration is in you, Mr Berry.

The door knocker is pounded.

Mr Berry (*with an urgency*) Don't answer it.

Mrs Berry Why not?

Mrs Berry opens the door.
    There is nobody there.
    Mr Berry is clearly relieved.
    Mrs Berry looks up and down the street. Noise offstage of youngsters shouting. Mrs Berry turns, arms folded.

Nobody.

Mr Berry Nobody . . . *Rien.*

Mrs Berry Why did you say don't answer it?

Mr Berry I thought it was that dimwit of a coalman – he brought the six bags of coal but not the timber, he said he'd be back with it . . . You know how he lingers for his slug of tea.

Mrs Berry But there was no horse and cart rumbling over the cobbles . . . no horse hooves . . . no yodel . . . he yodels, doesn't he? (*Looking at Mr Berry sharply.*) Are you running into debt – is it a debt collector you are hiding from?

Mr Berry What a bizarre idea.

Mrs Berry You got yourself a cashmere scarf and a bottle of vetiver – if that isn't bizarre, I don't know what is. On your meagre pension. (*Scrutinising.*) Say something.

Mr Berry Timber . . . I want dry timber, not the green sodden stuff . . . I told him, I told him that, and he shuffled off, said he'd have to go down to Kent to get it.

Mrs Berry (*serious*) Tell me that nothing of a financial nature is hovering over us? Tell me you are not going down to that bookmaker's again every single day, tell me that you have not hooked up with those scoundrels, those good-for-nothings, these loafers, Cassidy and Bullamore.

Mr Berry I've lost touch with them, no idea where they are. They could be in Australia.

Mrs Berry (*worried*) This is our little castle, Jack, this is all we have, and each other.

Mr Berry stares at her and as he does she is framed in the doorway by different panels of light, which become darker and darker until she seems a ghost.
Her image goes.

In her place, Hazel is standing in a wedding dress.
Mr Berry crosses to touch her.
The image fades.
Lights down.

Dusk in the room.
  The lamp is not lit.
  Knock on door offstage.
  Mr Berry comes in from kitchen, wiping his hands on
his butcher's apron.
  Second knock offstage.
  He hurries to the door.
  Hazel is holding a brightly coloured youth's chapan on
a pole. She is not wearing the beret, her long dark hair is
loose on her shoulders. She is excited.

Mr Berry But it's not Tuesday.

Hazel I know . . . I got it at a jumble sale and I thought
of you . . . I had to bring it.

  Mr Berry takes off his apron, puts it under cushion on
  Mrs Berry's chair and is clearly worried as Mrs Berry
  is presently due home from work.
  Hazel holds up the chapan proudly.

Mr Berry It's ravishing.

Hazel It's from Uzbekistan or Rajistan or somewhere
distant. They're called chapans. They were worn at
ceremonies.

Mr Berry And how old is our little chapan?

Hazel Very old . . . over a thousand years. If it could talk
it would tell us. (*She makes up the little story as she goes*

along.) Somewhere in China a family of silkworms were placed on wooden trays and fed the leaves of the white mulberry tree. They gorged. They ate like gluttons, they ate so much that they often had to sleep for a whole day before they began to eat again and from their juices they made a cocoon around their bodies. The cocoons were peeled off, the threads spun on a reel, then woven into cloth and dyed the richest colours, for an imperial prince. But there came wars and pestilence and it lay in a trunk for a long time. The trunk was stolen, brought overland into India and down the Ganges until at last it reached Constantinople and was sold at a bazaar to a merchant who bought it for a royal household. Hundreds more years went by until it found its way here to number 17B Formosa Lane.

She offers it to him somewhat ceremoniously.

Mr Berry (*drawing back*) Oh no.

Hazel Oh yes. You can frame it and hang it on your wall, that's what people do.

Mr Berry Let it be framed and hung on your wall.

Hazel But it's for here . . . to bring a bit of colour to the place.

Mr Berry Is the place so very colourless?

Hazel It's wintry.

Mr Berry Am I such a, a curmudgeon, hibernating?

Hazel Bound to. Living alone, no animal, no pet, I could pop in the odd Sunday and bring you crêpes from the Breton shop.

Mr Berry What a beacon of light you are.

Hazel Where will we hang it?

Mr Berry I'll have to think . . . Later on I'll do a design on paper, try different angles.

Hazel That's daft. (*She takes the chapan.*) If I hold it up, you can decide, hammer a few nails in.

Mr Berry turns away, head in his hands, stricken. He now has to feign illness.

What's wrong?

Pause.

Mr Berry (*pained*) Touch of the melancholia. Comes upon me . . . sense of . . . hopelessness . . . turning in on the self. (*He goes and draws the curtain.*) Nothing for it but to shut shop . . . Begging your pardon, Hazel, I must be alone.

Hazel Oh, poor Mr Berry.

Hazel hands him the chapan and goes.
    Mr Berry springs into action as Mrs Berry is due home. Clutching the chapan in one hand he draws back the curtains, wipes the sweat off his face with the chapan, closes the door, stands with his back to it, exhaling.

(*Agitated.*) 'Caveto be my counsellor.'

The door is pushed in abruptly and Mr Berry, on one foot, hops to avoid being knocked over.
    Mrs Berry enters carrying a bunch of dried lavender and sees him hobbling.

Mrs Berry Who are we this evening, Hopalong Cassidy?

Mr Berry (*feigning pain*) The growth, Gladys . . . the growth.

Mrs Berry looks, then biffs him with the lavender.

Mrs Berry Oh, poor muggins.

She sees the chapan and in a sharper tone addresses him.

What's that thing?

Mr Berry A chapan, it's called.

Mrs Berry grabs it.

Mrs Berry It's for a midget.

Mr Berry It's used in Asian ceremonies.

Mrs Berry Flapdoodle your Asian ceremonies, you're taking it right back – don't interrupt me, you're hatching in that Primavera day after day listening to those batty sisters, puffing you up with a false sense of your, ego and your superego. The place is passé, it's falling down. (*Smelling the chapan.*) Their stuff is musty.

Mr Berry Tush. Tush. I will return it.

Mr Berry waves the Madeira bottle.

Time for our tipple?

Pause.

Mrs Berry (*half conceding*) All right. I shall not break with tradition . . . the dear hour when working folk put their cares behind them.

Mr Berry The happy hour it's called nowadays . . . drinks at half price . . . cocktails. Bloody Mary . . . screwdriver.

Mrs Berry is silent and pondering, while he pours and while she has her first eager sips.

What would make you happy, Gladys? (*Pause.*) A house on Richmond Green? (*Pause.*) A pink Bentley? (*Pause.*) A cruise to the tombs of the Pharaohs?

Mrs Berry (*all of a sudden*) To be Jack and Gladys again and not Mr and Mrs Berry.

33

Mr Berry Nay, we are, we are.

Mrs Berry In the eyes of the world, yes, but not in our own private niche. (*Fixing him with her gaze.*) You redden . . . no need to redden, it's a fact of nature, men grow old and infirm far earlier than women. (*Authoritative.*) Why are there so many widows on the golf course, at every bridge table, in country women's associations up and down the land? Ask yourself, mutt.

Mr Berry (*tentative*) You wish me dead, is that it, Gladys?

Mrs Berry (*in full flow*) I wish you in Alpha . . . you are in Beta, Mr Berry, everything dropping, eyes, lizard eyelids, all your paraphernalia.

Mr Berry (*a bit surprised*) What is Alpha, my pet?

Mrs Berry (*imperious*) Close your eyes. (*More commanding.*) Close your eyes! (*Brisk.*) Look straight upwards, up up . . . look straight down . . . look to the right . . . look to the left. (*More brisk.*) Decisively . . . up to the left . . . down to the right . . . decisively, Mr Berry. Look to the left . . . look to the right.

Together Decisively.

Mrs Berry Up to the right . . . down to the left.

Together Decisively . . . decisively . . . decisively . . . decisively.
Mrs Berry Up . . . up

> *Mrs Berry takes his hand and together they repeat the exercise, saying the same word 'decisively' at different pitch, good humour restored. As their decisivelies become like a children's game, Mr Berry is impelled to rhyme.*

34

Mr Berry
'Up the airy mountain and down the rushy glen
We daren't go a-hunting for fear of little men,
Wee folk, good folk, trooping all together,
Green jacket, red cap and grey cock's feather!'

Mr Berry bends over, exhausted from his play acting.

Mrs Berry What a pretty verse . . . I haven't heard it in many a year.

Lights go down as good humour is restored.

SCENE FIVE

Night.
Mr Berry is seated, with a wooden tray on his lap. He is pouring seeds from packets into various compartments of the tray. He has a swivel lamp to see by.
Mrs Berry watches.
Silence.

Mrs Berry You're very quiet.

Mr Berry (*distant*) As befits the hour.

Mrs Berry What seeds are you sorting?

Mr Berry Oh . . . a variety.

Mrs Berry For a variety of occasions?

Mr Berry ignores the question, instead reads from one of the packets.

Mr Berry (*reading*) 'Plant outdoors in early spring as soon as soil can be worked. Keep moist until seedlings are established.'

Mrs Berry Keep moist until seedlings are established.

Mr Berry (*reading*) 'In frost-free climate, seeds may be planted earlier . . .'

Mrs Berry Keep moist! Have you noticed your wife's moist eyes of late?

> *Pause.*
>> *He does not reply.*

Two people under the same roof . . . under the same small roof . . . a wife crying and a husband wandering through the house . . . Why do you wander all night, as if you are looking for something or someone? What are you looking for?

Mr Berry (*evasive*) I don't know.

Mrs Berry One strategic difference. The wife knows why she is crying, the husband is, apparently . . . amnesiac.

Mr Berry (*irritable*) Oh, Gladys.

Mrs Berry Would the husband care to ask the cause of her tears?

Mr Berry You've always cried . . . it's one of your weapons.

Mrs Berry Something fishy happened today.

Mr Berry What . . . ?

Mrs Berry I came back at lunchtime and you were not here.

> *Mr Berry stops sorting.*

I took the bus . . . nobody home . . . your green velvet jacket not on its hanger.

Mr Berry I thought I told you that I was going to Carshalton . . . the second of my six appointments . . . A cold fish but very thorough, Mr Lawrence.

Mrs Berry I see. (*Turns towards kitchen then returns.*) You wear that jacket only for Christmas or our wedding anniversary. I even phoned Cooper. Brigadier Erica on reception said they had not seen you.

Mr Berry Hath not a man some privacy?

Mrs Berry Speak plainly, Mr Berry . . . this is a plain matter.

Mr Berry I took a stroll . . . I looked in the shop windows . . . I had a *café au lait* . . . Does that answer your question? (*With temper.*) I do not want to live in a totalitarian household. And that is final.

Mrs Berry All right, all right. It's just that I perceive a, a . . . gulf, an ever increasing gulf . . . here, in Versailles . . . last Sunday when we walked by the river . . . isn't it time we talked matters out?

Mr Berry Talk, talk . . . talk. We are not childhood sweethearts, we are not in the first flush of youth, we are not Romeo and Juliet.

Mrs Berry No . . . we are the warring what's-their-names families of Romeo and Juliet.

Mr Berry There is no war. (*Graver.*) We made a pact when I came back here . . . let us not break it.

Mrs Berry Threatening me, are you?

Mr Berry Boundaries. Boundaries that we do not cross . . . Man and wife or no man and wife . . . I can't stand it . . . I hate it, I recoil from these, interrogations . . . I can't breathe. I feel like, a, skinless animal . . . in a cage, in forty thousand cages.

Mrs Berry (*nervous*) What's wrong, Jack?

Mr Berry Nothing.

Mrs Berry When will you be your old self again?

Mr Berry I don't know.

Pause.
She picks up the seed packet and reads.

Mrs Berry 'Height twelve inches to eighteen . . . Cup-shaped flowers are so bright they almost glow.' (*Stands near him.*) Perhaps the holiday will bring us back to one another . . . The separation will do us good . . . time and space. Time to think of what you call, the verities.

Mr Berry Perhaps.

She puts her hand out.

Mrs Berry Frost-free. A truce, Mr Berry.

They shake hands, formally.
Mrs Berry goes to inner room.
Mr Berry continues sifting the seeds.
The silence is broken by the sound of Mrs Berry shouting offstage and drawers flung down.

(*Offstage.*) Denuded . . . my wardrobe is denuded.

Mrs Berry, ballistic, comes from inner room holding a cardboard box upside down; camphor balls roll along the stage.

The blue angora cardigan for Agadir is missing.

Mr Berry You probably brought it down to the thrift shop in your fluster.

Mrs Berry I did not bring it down to the thrift shop, I know I didn't. I've kept an inventory of everything I brought to the thrift shop. You've got to tell me.

Mr Berry (*cool*) I can't, I can't tell you.

Mrs Berry You're selling them, you're putting a nest egg away . . . you're plotting to leave me.

Mr Berry Calm down . . . your blood pressure will soar.

Mrs Berry Pass me that chair ere I faint . . . and get my smelling salts.

Mr Berry opens her handbag and hands her the bottle of smelling salts, which she inhales repeatedly.

It's a nightmare.

Mr Berry It's not a nightmare . . . it's a small thing . . . Look at the world around you, Gladys.

Mrs Berry I don't need to look at the world around me . . . I know the world . . . it's a web of lies and deceit. It's who is top dog and who is underdog . . . who is master and who is slave – (*shouting*) and who is pulling the wool over whose eyes.

Mrs Berry strides purposefully towards the inner room.
Mr Berry looks after her, has a few whiffs of the smelling salts and paces.
Mrs Berry returns with empty coat hangers and red velvet jewellery box.

(*Exclaiming.*) My black dress with the diamante clasp . . . my Balenciaga.

Mr Berry It was for when you were younger and more lissom . . . You haven't worn it in years.

Mrs Berry I could be lissom again . . . oh my God! (*Snapping open the velvet box.*) My rhinestone earrings . . . my seed pearls . . . It's . . . it's eerie. I'm calling the police.

Mr Berry No, Gladys . . . you are not calling the police. They wouldn't be interested.

Mrs Berry They will have seen someone loitering about here . . . a stranger.

Mr Berry It's the ruffians from the flats . . . they sneak around the back . . . they know the ropes . . . they watch for when I go out.

Mrs Berry The police can search those flats.

Mr Berry They'll have sold them already.

Pause.

Mrs Berry There's something rotten in this house of Versailles. Out with it.

Mr Berry goes behind the screen and fetches two glasses and the bottle of Madeira, waves it, much to her chagrin. He pours, he drinks rapidly. She does not drink, but watches him keenly.

Mr Berry I gave them to someone.

Mrs Berry (*aghast*) A woman.

Mr Berry Cassidy . . . he had no one else in the world to turn to . . . terrible debts . . . can't quit the gambling . . . can't lick it . . . On the way to the river, to drown himself.

Mrs Berry You and Cassidy sold them?

Mr Berry We had to.

Mrs Berry Oh my God, my edge-to-edge, my Rio Ritas, my rhinestone earrings, my Balenciaga . . . How could you, how could you?

Mr Berry He had to find the fifty quid or the family would be evicted.

Mrs Berry Fifty quid! Is that all they fetched?

Mr Berry He's going to write to you . . . he's going to send you flowers.

Mrs Berry I don't want flowers. I want my treasures back, my seersucker dress and my pencil skirt and my cardigan, every single thing had a significance. It's the callousness, the inhumanity, I feel crushed in heart and soul.

Mr Berry I'll make it up to you. I'll replenish your wardrobe.

Mrs Berry On what? On what . . .? Where did you sell them?

Mr Berry Greenwich . . . the woman gave us a lump sum . . . she had a purchaser in mind.

Mrs Berry (*thoughtful*) So that's what it is?

Mr Berry (*quietly*) Yes.

Mrs Berry But . . . why my wardrobe and not yours?

Mr Berry I did part with my watch.

Mrs Berry Your gold watch, your gold hunter with the foliate flowers and the Roman numerals, your birthright.

Mr Berry nods, then sits holding his head in his hands. Pause.

Oh, Jack Berry, what a softie you are.

Mr Berry I'll get you an angora cardigan. I saw a very nice one in Genevieve's on the High Street.

Mrs Berry You won't.

Mr Berry I swear. (*Quoting from the Book of Common Prayer.*) 'All at once came terror in their dreams, each fallen where fall he must, they confessed whose fault it was and . . . they expiated.'

Mrs Berry And you've been plucking up the courage to tell me.

Mr Berry Yes.

Mrs Berry You didn't want to hurt me.

Mr Berry Yes, I mean no.

Mrs Berry I suppose that's love . . . that is what is called love, by the Seers and the Bard.

She drinks, smacks her lips, drinks more.

(*Mellowed somewhat.*) Do you remember on one of our Sunday strolls when we were courting, the Fair Isle jumper in the pharmacy window . . . we thought it odd to see it in the pharmacy . . . it had the name of the lady who had knitted it, Fiona . . . Fiona something . . . You never told me . . . you never uttered a word . . . week after week you put a five-shilling deposit down . . . then Christmas you left it on the table with the little fluffy red powder puff and we danced and we danced . . . Oh, Solomon, why don't Solomon and Sheba go dancing any more?

Mr Berry, relieved at how things have transpired, leads her into a slow waltz.

I put it on and walked around the bedsitter in my bloomers . . . you had the little fluffy red powder puff . . . for your ruses . . . (*Imitating his voice.*) 'Let me take you a buttonhole or two lower, madam.' (*Her own voice.*) And jealous . . . the jealousies . . . fuming that night in the Catherine Wheel when the actors pressed me to sing 'Eileen Aroon' . . . I sang 'Eileen Aroon'. (*Thinks.*) The rose bush you put down for me . . . 'old blush' . . . near where our little cocker spaniel is buried.

Mr Berry Little Biscuit.

She stops the dance.

Mrs Berry Was it your fault, Jack, or mine that we didn't have that child?

Mr Berry Don't, dearest.

Mrs Berry We should have been abstinent . . . that she or that he would be here now amidst us. We had names . . . I favoured Aubrey and you wanted Iseult, from the myth.

Mr Berry It was twenty-eight years ago.

Mrs Berry We were sure it had, settled in . . . meshed, that it would not miscarry. The pains all of a sudden on the number 14 bus . . . like knives, scores of knives going through me, people moving away appalled. I sat on that bus seat alone, stuck to it.

Mr Berry (*assuaging*) It's in heaven.

Mrs Berry (*emphatic*) We went to Versailles when we shouldn't have . . . you couldn't get enough of me . . . in those days . . . in my blush-rose days, Jack St John Berry.

She sobs and he holds her in his arms.
   Lights go down.

SCENE SIX

Two figures, Hazel and Mr Berry, in dim light, the elocution lesson just finishing. Mr Berry repeats lines from Othello.

Mr Berry (*from Othello*)
                              'I did consent,
And often did beguile her of her tears,
When I did speak of some distressful stroke
That my youth suffered: my story being done,
She gave me for my pains a world of sighs.'

Lights come up, Hazel somewhat abstracted.
   A white cake box with a red ribbon on the table.
   Mr Berry picks it up and bows to thank her.

Most kind.

Hazel We have to finish early.

Mr Berry What is it? What's wrong?

Hazel I've nowhere to live.

Mr Berry Nowhere to live!

Hazel The landlord, Raymond, promised Mother that he'd never throw us out . . . never . . . She worked for him . . . she did all the sewing and she found him things at auctions, tapestries and things like that . . . He always said she had the best eye . . . I have to find a room.

Mr Berry There's rooms everywhere in London, rooms, penthouses, studios, all across the city, people travelling or getting divorced, houses empty.

Hazel I know.

Mr Berry What you want is a mews house, a mews house in a row of similar houses painted a washed pink or a washed yellow, tubs of flowers, cobblestones, neighbours at one with one another, Sunday morning drinks, carol singing at Christmas time –

Hazel (*cutting in*) A week's notice . . . the letter was slipped under my bedroom door . . . His chauffeur has a key . . . he inspects all the flats . . . I tried calling but Mr Raymond wouldn't come to the phone, even if he'd said 'I'm raising the rent' it wouldn't be so bad . . . Instead of that some spiel about major dilapidation, none of the other tenants had an envelope slipped in under the door concerning major dilapidation. I had it for a song, I suppose it was charity and he has no more charity left in him.

Mr Berry I would say come here, were it not for Bullamore.

Hazel Who's Bullamore?

44

Mr Berry Bit of a rake . . . decamped the week before last.

Hazel I never hear him.

Mr Berry Shhh.

He takes her arm and leads her downstage.

(*Whispering.*) Sleeps all day . . . works in a nightclub somewhere in West Kensington . . . can't be top-drawer because he is both doorman and croupier . . . not hoi polloi . . . came here out of the blue . . . an altercation with a landlady, I imagine.

Hazel I have to go, Mr Berry . . . I have to look at two places.

Mr Berry A father, Hazel . . . is there not a father?

Hazel (*shaking her head*) I never knew him . . . Mother never spoke of him . . . a fly-by-night.

Mr Berry How I wish I could shelter you, Hazel.

Hazel runs out.
Mr Berry stands centre stage, thoughtful.
Mrs Berry comes with the customary handbag, her hair as always perfectly pinnacled and secured with headscarf.

Mrs Berry Why are you standing there mooning?

Mr Berry (*with charm*) The spring, the spring, so infectious, the earth yielding forth its favours . . . purple and white crocuses by Mary-le-Bow, saw them on my sallies.

Mrs Berry And what of the interview with Messrs Gross and Kandinsky?

Mr Berry Pipped to the post.

Mrs Berry (*with sarcasm*) Astonishing.

Mrs Berry enters and he helps her take off her coat.

Mr Berry How was today, dear?

Mrs Berry (*pushing him in*) Same as yesterday . . . same as every day . . . You ask this fatuous question, 'How was today, dear?' and you don't give a fig. You have no idea what I have to endure in that place, young girls, whippersnappers . . . laughing at me behind my back . . . and targets, having to meet targets.

Mr Berry You're supervisor, you're boss.

Mrs Berry I still answer to the powers that be. (*Anxious.*) I daren't fail . . . I dare not.

Mr Berry They esteem you.

Mrs Berry Huh! (*Pause.*) I inspect each and every dolly, make sure they're dressed prettily, their frocks or their sailor suits, their undies, shoes and socks, bonnets for the girls, caps for the boys. It falls to me to do the most exacting task of all, to glue on the hair and the eyelashes. The eyelashes are an art in itself, you see, they must flutter, and no two flutters are alike . . . they must be unique and they must be fetching . . . little temptresses. We're getting an award. Who were you expecting?

Mr Berry Nobody. An award . . . that's a feather in your cap.

Mrs Berry Yes, 'By Appointment to Her Majesty'. (*More alert.*) So you were turned down again.

Mr Berry There will be lots of work in the parks later on, lots of planting, the begonias, the hostas, the hollyhocks for the summer fetes.

Mrs Berry You lack incentive. You don't want work, you eschew it.

Mr Berry I am a sick man.

Mrs Berry looks down at the open book beside the cake box. She reads.

Mrs Berry 'The funeral baked meats did coldly furnish forth the marriage table.' What cakes are these?

Mr Berry (*testy*) I don't know.

Mrs Berry, somewhat thrown by this, picks up the cake box and walks around with it, not quite knowing where to put it.
Pause.

I know how you worry . . . I worry too . . . I *hate* this limbo.

Mrs Berry The humours get the better of me, the bile . . .

Mr Berry Only vestigially.

Mrs Berry Vestigially . . . I like that, I shall use it on my whippersnappers, you could fit their vocabulary into a matchbox . . . I shall keep my harangues for them.

Mr Berry And I shall leave no stone unturned. What would you say, Gladys, if we were to adopt somebody?

Mrs Berry Adopt? Jeepers creepers, we're past our prime . . . being wakened up at night . . . teething, toddling.

Mr Berry Not a baby . . . an adult.

Mrs Berry What type of adult?

Mr Berry Someone pleasing . . . with a softening influence.

Mrs Berry A member of the fair sex?

Mr Berry Yes, a daughter.

Mrs Berry (*bristling*) Why not a son, an Aubrey? I know why, you want one of the whippersnapper ilk to tickle your fancy. How you plot and scheme to humiliate me . . .

Mr Berry You had such a lovely nature once . . . after the honeymoon you put pieces of wedding cake into small white boxes for men and women both, you didn't have a shred of jealousy.

Mrs Berry I had no occasion to.

Mr Berry You wrote letters describing the big day . . . you were magnanimous . . . you would have welcomed strangers, any stray could put his or her head down, you wouldn't turn a soul away . . . It's what I loved in you . . . the magnanimity.

Mrs Berry With so much gone, what's left, Mr Berry? What's left?

Pause.
Mr Berry goes.
Mrs Berry walks back and forth, clasping both arms, a bit shivery.

Some trollop . . . in the attic . . . in her lingerie, humming . . . It's a fad, it's a passing fad. (*Quiet.*) No. The gulf's not widened. (*Thoughtful.*) This calls for . . . mercy, a sweetness. (*Confident.*) Have I not heard a thousand times, 'I'll never leave you Gladys'? And so it is. The fuel's not gone that fed the fire.

Darkness.

SCENE SEVEN

Happy hurdy-gurdy music offstage as from a funfair.
Mr Berry at one side of the stage, dressing for an outing. He fixes a spotted dicky-bow in an imaginary mirror, then tries on a panama hat, removes it and re-dons it at a rakish angle.
At the opposite side of the stage Hazel is putting the finishing touches to her attire. She buttons her black

jacket, then steps into very high-heeled black court shoes,
first one, then the other.
  As the lights come up an old-fashioned carousel
descends on gilded ropes.

Mr Berry Hazel's gloves . . . Hazel's basket . . . Hazel's
eyes. She did not know how happy she made me and she
was not meant to know. Treason, stratagems and spoils.

Hazel (*calling across*) I like your hat.

Mr Berry She was brimming with happiness. She'd found
a place . . . I helped. Grandfather's hunter watch fetched
far more than I could have hoped for. Chap in Bond
Street most impressed, said there had only been a few
dozen ever made, the way he put it was, it was like a
wine from a very exclusive vineyard. She hesitated about
taking the money and got a ruled notepad to write her
IOUs . . . Here in Whitstable . . . home of the oyster.

  Sound offstage of music, crashing waves and yelping
  of a dog.
  The scene is played with their walking, side by side,
  at other times facing each other, yet again Hazel
  running, throwing one of her shoes to the dog.
  Mr Berry sometimes talks to the audience and
  sometimes to Hazel. Likewise Hazel's dialogue is
  disjointed and in answer to questions of his that the
  audience has not heard.

Mr Berry Gave me a tour of the little flat. It did not look
onto the sea but the sea was contiguous to it. Most
bracing. Small room with a terrace. She said she would
get wooden washtubs and plant her favourite flowers.

Hazel Lily of the valley, freesia, violas and sweet pea.

Mr Berry Walking along the pier she told me the Kipling
story. Stayed up reading the night before – a woman lost
an only child, grief-stricken . . . empty house, empty

passages. One evening when she opened the casement window she heard sounds in the garden, the lilts of children in the garden . . . a whole flock of children . . . ghosts. (*Holding his arms out.*) Big wild waves foam twenty feet high, swept off our feet.

Over Hazel's next speech the lights of the carousel come on.

Hazel (*as if in answer to a question*) The landlady. She's moody, she's foreign . . . her cousins come most evenings . . . they have red cabbage with Wiener schnitzel . . . The lodgers must cook their suppers early and take them to their rooms . . . we can't even look at her saucepans or her utensils.

Mr Berry Everything static . . . the swings . . . the bucket chair . . . the long golden manes of the rocky horses, until she touched one and all of a sudden the whole thing came alive and moved and she moved with it, the dais, the roped pillars, the haughty horses going round and round.

Over his last speech Hazel has got on one of the rocking horses and is already singing, her song bound up with his words.

Hazel (*singing*)
    'I know where I'm going,
    And I know who's going with me.
    I know who I love,
    And my dear knows who I'll marry.

    I have stockings of silk,
    And shoes of bright green leather,
    Combs to buckle my hair,
    And a ring for every finger.

    Oh, feather beds are soft,
    And painted rooms are bonnie,
    But I would give them all,
    For my handsome winsome Johnny.

Some say that he's poor,
But I say that he's bonnie,
Fairest of them all,
Is my handsome, winsome Johnny.'

(*The speaking voice of a conductor.*) All aboard.

Mr Berry, too shy to get on, waves self-consciously.
Hazel gets down from the rocking horse and they
walk this way and that.

Mr Berry The coast to ourselves . . . our footprints in the
wet sand . . . hers, daintier than mine . . . following upon
one another . . . A feeling of – (*searching for the word*) of
buoyancy . . . buoyant . . . waves soaking my shoes, my
shoelaces.

Hazel Take them off.

Mr Berry A dog followed us . . . she threw things to it . . .
she called him Charlie.

Hazel Our Charlie was a mongrel . . . people drove him
and left him blindfold at the funfair . . . dumped him . . .
In the evening when everyone had packed up . . . he was
still there, he wasn't even crying, he was that frightened,
that browbeaten, we couldn't leave him, it turned out he
was the best dog ever, he'd nearly talk to you. I can't
understand anyone dumping a dog, can you? (*Happier
voice.*) Charlie, Charlie.

Mr Berry The dog tripped her and I had to catch her
before she fell . . . (*He does.*) My hands caught her and
held her and all was fluxion and all was fire.

Hazel withdraws from his clasp.

Hazel (*excited*) Yes, I *am* hungry.

Mr Berry The tea house all to ourselves . . . seating for
a hundred . . . not a soul . . . the spray smack up against

the window pane . . . couldn't see out . . . like being on
an ocean liner . . . it happened so suddenly . . . tears . . .
tears . . . unbearable sadness . . . some trigger . . . the big
wild waves or maybe the dog . . . or the saffron buns . . .
or the child's high chair at the end of the restaurant . . .
red beads . . . red abacus . . . such tears . . . I could have
cupped them . . . I wanted to hold her . . . tell her she
was not alone . . . except that she was. I had to restrain
myself . . . hold my feelings in . . . make do . . . like a
patient, on a drip. (*Colluding voice.*) But I was happy,
happy to be with her, happy to know that some thread
now joined us together. A golden chain. After she came
back from the powder room she blurted it out. The
mother had had to put her away for the first five years,
had regretted it all their lives . . . the first five years in
some institution.

Hazel (*unemotional*) I was called Mary there . . . my
name was Mary then.

> *Hazel hands Mr Berry a large pink seashell and backs
> away, carrying her shoes.*
> *She goes.*
> *Mr Berry puts the shell to his ear as he stoops in
> front of one of the tiny mirrors that front the carousel.
> He puts the shell in his pocket, then removes the
> dicky-bow while whistling the air of the song she sang.*
> *Lights of carousel fade as it swings upwards and out
> of view.*
> *As he walks his exuberance lessens.*

Mr Berry Gladys was incandescent with rage . . . Where
had I been? Why hadn't I left a note? Did I not realise
that she would be thinking the worst? That I'd had a
heart attack on the underground, or in the underpass and
left for dead . . . terror in her eyes, thinking that I had left
for good, because I'd threatened to.

> *Glaring light in room.*

Searched my pockets . . . found the docket . . . one coach
ticket London–Whitstable return . . . teas for two . . .
I said it was Bullamore. He had wind of a job coming up
for me in Merton Park, she roared with laughter . . . her
eyes boring right through me . . . but I was drunk, drunk
with happiness. She went across, took the coins out of
the jug, off out into the lane without hat or coat at that
hour . . . down to the public kiosk . . . to phone Iris . . .
to collude.

I should have guessed, but my cup, it brimmeth over.

Lights go down.

SCENE EIGHT

Lights come up.
*Mr Berry carrying two large gaudy suitcases from inner
room to doorway. He kneels to secure them with straps.*
*Mrs Berry comes from the inner room in coat and
elaborate picture hat with fruits, flowers and gauze and
diamanté-winged dark glasses, which she takes on and
off depending on her needs.*
*The scene is bustling with excitement and over it there
are the beeps from a waiting motorcar.*

Mrs Berry Ducky, can you open it . . .? I can't remember
if I put in my feather boa.

Mr Berry You won't need it – the temperature is in the
high seventies . . . according to *The Times*.

Mrs Berry Just to be on the safe side . . . in case of a
draught . . . at dinner.

Mr Berry You're bringing far too much.

Mrs Berry I know, I know . . . I'm all butterflies . . . I
didn't sleep a wink . . . We're not sure if it's dressing down

or dressing up . . . and not having an escort, Iris says it's a shame . . . Oh yes, and she wondered if you would like Fred to pop around on Sunday for company . . . he goes to the War Museum . . . he's still writing that dissertation on weaponry.

Mr Berry I can't stand hearing about wars and weaponry.

Mrs Berry That's what I said . . . but I sugared the pill . . . I said you'd be busy . . . pottering and mulching . . . you will be mulching, won't you?

Mr Berry Most definitely.

Mrs Berry Me, awake all night wondering, will the food agree with us, will Iris be pulling a long face, will they meet us off the plane and might they speak a word of English.

Mr Berry But you have the dictionary . . .

Car beeps.

Mrs Berry It's a shame you're not coming . . . a gentleman at the table makes all the difference in those cultures . . . adds cachet. (*In answer to the beeps.*) Oh, do shut up . . . And don't forget Friday's appointment.

Mr Berry I won't.

Mrs Berry roots in the suitcase, checking for her stole.

Mrs Berry Found it.

She pulls out a pink feather boa, dangles it, puts it back, as Mr Berry kneels to close the case.
Sound of beeps more insistent.

Mr Berry Mind you get on the right part of the train for Gatwick . . . they shuttle bits off . . . be sure to ask the conductor.

Mrs Berry (*effusive*) For your dinner this evening there's shepherd's pie and you have pork chops and gravy tomorrow . . . cauliflower cheese for starter . . . all in the larder. My darling . . . you should be with us . . . the gardens are apparently . . . a feature . . . You would get inspiration . . . bring back cuttings, ferns, shade-loving plants and rare flowers. Coming.

> *She gives him a peck and goes out, he follows with the suitcases.*
> *Lights go down.*

SCENE NINE

Room with candlelight.
> *A nostalgic tune from a music box, which comes on and off intermittently.*
> *Dark curtain drawn over the window.*
> *Mr Berry in maroon velvet jacket.*
> *Hazel's coat and rush bag on table.*
> *Hazel in lace wedding dress with myriad covered buttons down the front and on either sleeve.*

Mr Berry Enchanting . . . or should I say, enchant-ed.

Hazel It's a very lovely lace and very rare.

Mr Berry It was in the family for generations . . . Mother said it came from Spain, on one of the ships of the Armada. Mother loved making up romantic stories.

Hazel What was she like?

Mr Berry Oh, very beautiful and trusting and wounded. After my father left she shut herself off from the world, she would sit in the morning room with her spaniel, staring out the window, Tom, the old retainer, used to write to me . . . She wouldn't touch food . . . drank barley water . . . Of course I was young then, and careless.

Hazel shivers.

Are you cold?

Hazel (*touching the dress*) Yes, it's freezing.

Mr Berry It's bound to feel cold, in that trunk for years and years. I'm surprised it's not frozen over with dew and mildew. (*Animated.*) But you'll warm it, Hazel . . . the way you warm this room . . . the way you illuminate the universe. How about a little celebration . . . a glass of Madeira?

Hazel Only a sip.

Mr Berry The veil and the gloves are on the bureau.

Hazel goes through velvet curtain.
  Mr Berry, waving a full bottle of Madeira, walks and talks as he pours.

(*To the audience.*) Not a kink . . . no Gladys . . . enchantment . . . the precipice . . . a coming-home, even to the edge of ruin. (*As she returns.*) What shall we drink to, Hazel? Love, honour, Alexander Blok . . . St Petersburg in the snows?

Hazel holding up the veil.

Hazel It's full of holes . . . you could strain milk through it, and the tiara is yellowed, orange blossom – (*she smells it*) and maybe, myrtle.

Mr Berry (*softly*) Put them on.

Hazel puts on the veil.

(*Enraptured.*) This shall be my St Crispin's Day.

They drink.

He wouldn't look away now . . . in the elevator . . . *la chasse* . . . the chase . . . Daphne holds the reins where

56

Apollo must follow . . . up the aisle . . . bestrewn with orange blossom . . . the strains of the medieval fugue.

Hazel You're a caution, Mr Berry.

Mr Berry You still wait, Hazel . . . I know by your eyes.

Hazel (*slightly impatient*) I can't linger . . . it's a long way from here . . . it's out in Petersham.

She doesn't sit, which flusters him.

Mr Berry And you are playing a bride?

Hazel I'm playing a woman that's a little gone in the head. Mary Tyrone. In the play she actually carries the wedding dress, she walks around, trailing it, her mind all fog, she doesn't even see her husband or her sons. Then she has this vision of when she was praying in the shrine of Our Lady of Lourdes and promised to be a nun. (*Quoting from* Long Day's Journey.) 'Then in the spring something happened to me. Yes, I remember. I fell in love with James Tyrone and was so happy for a time.'

Mr Berry A vision. Do you have visions, Hazel?

Hazel (*with a shiver*) I'd be afraid to.

Mr Berry (*reflective*) I was over Battersea way . . . can't remember why . . . oh yes, I do . . . it was in answer to a vacancy for a park keeper . . . I was passed over . . . Walking back it began to rain . . . showers at first, then a downpour . . . the heavens opened . . . I took shelter in a summerhouse . . . everything began to go green, not a pleasant green, more a peculiar, brooding green. The grass, the leaves, the tree trunks and my eyesight grew green also and then it went black, all went pitch black and I had this, well, not strictly a vision, not like Mary Tyrone but yet again similar to Mary Tyrone in that I entered a haze, a sort of no-man's-land, quite alone . . . at the end of my tether . . . Outside, out in the world that

57

is, there were two of everything, of every sort of bird and
beast and fowl and man and woman, male and female
joined together and I had this wish, more like a curse
than a wish, I wished doom on all of them, with all my
heart I wished that the world would come to an end at
that moment, that everything, the ducks in the pond, the
park, the River Thames that I was staring at, the big flats
along the Embankment and beyond that the streets and
the buses and the cars and the car parks, men and
machines and the fowls of the air, the creeping things, the
Queen's swans, all, all wiped out and I with them, because
there seemed to be nothing, only the void. (*Pause, then
perking up.*) It was a passing thing . . . I wouldn't have it
now . . . not with the way things have turned out . . .
a sort of hallucination. I would not want the world ended
now, not with all that has happened.

He is staring at her.
Hazel runs her hand over the sleeves of the dress.

Hazel My friend Sally will wash this for you . . . she
wraps the garments in muslin and washes the whole
thing, then irons them half wet. It will be like new.

Mr Berry I was wondering, I was wondering, Hazel, if
I might come with you, incognito of course, well out of
sight . . . somewhere in the back row.

Hazel Mr Berry, it's not in a theatre, it's in a hospice,
people dying.

Mr Berry (*ignoring that*) Came on a very enticing
address up in Mayfair – I had some business there – not
quite a restaurant, not quite a pub, more a salon, so
informal, sofas, cushions, nooks for privacy, nooks shut
off with beaded curtains, art deco lamps, steeped in
atmosphere, the sort of place where one can have a bite,
talk. (*More intimate.*) You know, Hazel, talk, let one's
hair down, those moments of . . . *tendresse.*

Hazel No, Quincy.

Mr Berry (*slightly crushed*) No?

Hazel It's a birthday party for an old woman. Barnaby is doing Tommy Cooper and there's step dancing and a singsong and me. Then tea and cake.

Mr Berry I haven't seen step dancing in years . . . it's so vigorous, so animated, girls or boys or mixed, they wear what is called a crios, a knitted belt with numerous medals, proudly suspended from the waist.

Hazel Only staff and close relatives are invited.

Mr Berry Most sorry . . . an aberration. (*Formal.*) It was only a matter of a moment, a split second, a suggestion –

Hazel (*cutting in*) It wasn't. It was letting our hair down, *tendresse.* (*Urgent.*) Unrequited love can unhinge a person.

Mr Berry (*quashed*) I . . . understand.

Hazel (*sincere*) You've been like a father to me.

A shadow of a figure outside the window.

Mr Berry May I hear Mary Tyrone's words again?

Hazel There's someone at the window.

Mr Berry It's the roughs from the flats . . . Just one more time . . . just so as I don't forget it.

Hazel (*as Mary Tyrone*) 'Then in the spring something happened to me. Yes, I remember. I fell in love with James Tyrone and was so happy for a time.'

The knocks on the window loud, insistent.
Mr Berry rushes across and lifts the curtain.

Mr Berry (*frantic*) It's my wife, my wife . . . take it off.

Hazel I thought she was dead.

Mr Berry In God's name take it off . . . I shall unravel all . . . Just take it off.

Mrs Berry (*offstage*) Open that door, Jack Berry.

Hazel (*incredulous*) Jack . . . Quincy . . . Bullamore?

Mr Berry (*pleading*) I was in that summerhouse in Battersea Park, I swear it, and I did curse and I did weep and I did gnash, you must believe me.

Hazel I do.

The large key falls onto the floor as Mrs Berry has picked the lock from the outside.

Mr Berry Oh, Christ. Keep calm, Hazel, she gets quite intemperate, quite histrionic, my wife does.

He throws off the maroon jacket and Hazel struggles with the buttons on the cuffs of the wedding dress.
Door flung open and Mrs Berry in her holiday attire comes in, the hat askew.

Mrs Berry (*almost gleeful*) Ah, for whom the bell tolls, it tolls for thee, Jack St John Berry, you fool you, you fool, believing that I would have gone away, that I was blind to the signs and the portents . . . I can trace it to the very first flutter . . . one of those moments of pure clairvoyance . . . the Tuesday that you announced your growth, your phantom growth. (*To Hazel.*) Who are you?

Hazel (*not looking up*) Hazel.

Mrs Berry What are you doing in my wedding dress?

Hazel I thought you were dead.

Mrs Berry laughs wildly, hysterically.

Mrs Berry Dead. Nice. Nice. 'The funeral baked meats did coldly furnish forth the marriage table.' Dead, am I? And you are here to take my place . . . to step into my shoes, but where pray is the silver coach and the glass slippers? Spun you a yarn, did he, a fairy tale. He's a dreamer . . . do you know what a dreamer is . . .? A dreamer has scaled the Matterhorn, a dreamer has sat at the world's top tables, a dreamer has played Shakespeare in his birthplace and comes from a wealthy Anglo-Irish family on the estuary . . . money no object, rolling in it . . . venerable family crest, thoroughbreds, hounds, lurchers – (*more common voice*) buckets in the hallway to catch the rain . . . his mother in and out of the loony bin . . . a dreamer sends his wife to work while he prowls the High Street in his cravat in search of a bit of skirt. (*Vicious.*) On the game, are you?

Mr Berry (*trying to be reasonable*) These are wild and ranting words, Gladys. You are letting yourself down.

Mrs Berry Fie on you. What woman wouldn't? Traitor. Adulterer. (*She sights the two drinks.*) The nec-tar of deceit – (*She drinks one fast and resumes her tirade.*) What woman wouldn't . . . in my position . . .? (*She picks up the second glass.*) A slut in my wedding dress . . . the raiment of my marriage vows . . . Of course it takes two to tango. (*Going towards Hazel.*) Why did you pick him? You came here again and again to rifle my wardrobe, abuse my hospitality, break into my hard-won happiness, and why do you stand there brazen as brass, enrobed in what is not yours but is mine . . . mine.

Mr Berry You shall have it back.

Mrs Berry It's tainted, it's contaminated.

> *Mrs Berry downs the second glass in a gulp, Hazel meanwhile has one arm freed of the dress.*
>   *Mrs Berry is intoxicated now.*

What has he promised you? Flight. A midnight dash across the English Channel . . . star-crossed lovers, travelling incognito from canton to canton . . . sleeping in the straw . . . having to beg for bread . . . You don't seem to me to be a person of means. (*Picking up Hazel's rush basket and examining it.*) You seem to me to be rather skint. (*Throws the handbag down.*) Cast-offs. Came upon him in the Primavera, did you, buying that stupid panama hat that made him look like a correspondent in a farce – oh the palaver, the palavering, afternoon tea in the Polish place where they have the free newspapers, bamboozled you with apple strudel and flattery . . . strewing gifts in your way, my jewels were not enough, his gold hunter watch that was his only heirloom had to be pawned to pay for your greediness. There is a word for women like you and it is not a nice word and you know it. (*Fierce now.*) Say it say it say it. Whore whore whore.

Mr Berry Stop it, Gladys. You insult a lady.

Mrs Berry (*shouting*) Poppycock.

Mr Berry (*shouting*) A lady.

Mrs Berry Choose then. Choose between one lady and th' other, between tried and untried mettle. (*She grasps Hazel's arm.*)

Hazel (*terrified*) Let go of me.

Mrs Berry Watch him – (*searching for the word*) tremble. (*To him.*) Bewail your downfall. (*Soaring.*) To be deceived, to be betrayed, to be out-matrimonied by a traitor.

Mr Berry It's not what you think, Gladys.

Mrs Berry Excuse me. It's not what I think? It's what I think and more. How come I am pronounced dead? Dead.

Mr Berry I never touched her.

Mrs Berry (*stunned*) You never touched her . . . that's worse.

She has to pause to absorb this piece of news.
Hazel turns to go behind the screen to take off the dress.
Mrs Berry is now out of control.

Dream on. Her youth, her beauty, her lustre, her maidenhood . . . serenade beneath her casement window. (*Vicious.*) I'll kill her.

Mrs Berry grabs the secateurs, snaps at the air as she goes to hack the veil.
Hazel lets out a gasp of terror.
Mr Berry pulls Mrs Berry back and they fight, the secateurs caught between them, Mrs Berry shouting heated but inaudible curses at him.
Hazel passes behind them, grabbing her coat and her handbag.
Mr Berry gets the better of the fight, as Mrs Berry loses her balance and falls to the floor.
She lies there, believing he will help her up, but he doesn't.
Mr Berry follows to the open door where Hazel has gone out.

Mr Berry Stay . . . stay.

Mrs Berry (*furious*) Stay? Stay?

Mrs Berry makes quite a show of getting up.
Mr Berry by the open door is shouting excitedly.

Mr Berry Vanna manna famma namma up the airy mountain and down the rushy glen we daren't go a-hunting for fear of little men. (*Different tone.*) Big high waves. And the rocky horses rearing to go . . . Charlie Charlie . . . (*More impassioned.*)

'I send you a cream-white rosebud,
With a flush on its petal tips,
For the love that is purest and sweetest,
Has a kiss of desire on the lips.'

Mrs Berry is pulling him back with all her might.

Mrs Berry Have you gone mad?

Mrs Berry pulls him in and slams the door.

Mr Berry (*with a cold smile*) Mad. Yes.

Mrs Berry stares at him, then goes to the inner room.
Mr Berry opens the door, looks out, retreats to the rocking chair, holding the secateurs. He opens and shuts the two forks repeatedly, venting his anger.
The door creaks in.
He looks up with evident hope.
The wedding dress is left on the floor and in the gusts of wind it billows across the stage, where it will remain.
Mrs Berry returns from the bedroom, her hair wild, her bravura gone.
She stands behind him.

Mrs Berry You have to tell me, I have to know what's in your heart.

Mr Berry, still wielding the secateurs, does not reply.
Mrs Berry waits, then takes the doll from the shelf, holds it, looks at it, presses its belly and the doll goes 'bahbahbah'. Repeated 'bahbahbahs'.

Hold me, Jack.

Pause.

You don't have to tell me . . . you don't have to say anything . . . Just hold me . . . like you done on the Black Mountain. (*In a desperate whisper.*) Hold me.

He doesn't move.
Mrs Berry goes.
Slow darkness.
Intermittent 'bahbah' from doll on shelf.

SCENE TEN

Morning light.
Mr Berry, holding the watering can, about to go
behind the glass wall.
Hazel enters from the street. She looks different, more
unkempt, a short dirndl skirt and red wedge-heeled
platform shoes. She speaks in two different voices, either
a drawl from deep down, the consequence of medication,
and at other times a light tinkling voice.
Mr Berry stands, takes one step, then hesitates as Hazel
crosses to where the doll is.

Hazel Hello, Dolly.

She touches its belly and the doll goes 'bahbah'. She
picks it up, cradles it with a tenderness, half sings, half
speaks her lullaby.

Ba-ba black sleep, have you any wool?
Yes sir, yes sir, three bags full,
One for the master and one for the dame
And one for the little boy who lives down the lane.

Mr Berry Hazel.

Hazel (*odd voice*) How are *you*, Mr Berry?

Hazel puts the doll down, walks towards him, lifts
from inside her sweater a plastic ID card on a string,
with her name and photograph, holds it up for him
to see.

That's me. My pass. (*Scolding voice.*) Back at teatime,
Hazel . . . Big house in its own grounds . . . guard dogs.

> *She then shows him the whistle that is attached and
> mimes blowing into it.*

Case I get lost or go roaming in the gloaming.

Mr Berry Where would that be, Hazel?

Hazel Further north . . . chap mows the lawn . . . Aziz,
Aziz . . . little goatee beard . . . puts down the pet-un-ias.
(*Colluding voice.*) Leaves the hose on all night . . . I hear
it trick-ling . . . trick-ling.

Mr Berry How did you get here?

Hazel We motored . . . Nurse Bracken is waiting outside
in the car. (*Mimes it.*) Having a fag. Went to a posh
place where they keep the records – wills and birth
certificates . . . (*She giggles.*) Divorce and adoption. Got
my papers . . . my pedigree.

Mr Berry I have wondered about your . . . your
whereabouts.

Hazel What would you like for Christmas, Mr Berry?

Mr Berry It's not Christmas for ages.

Hazel We're knitting like crazy . . . (*She mimes the
knitting.*) Socks . . . and . . . pullovers. (*Confidential.*)
They asked who was my next of kin and I said you was
my nuncle . . . A fib . . . they know now . . . not a bad
sort. Bracken . . . she has a teeny moustache.

Mr Berry Can I help, Hazel? With . . . money or . . .

Hazel (*grandiose*) The state keeps me . . . Like King or
Queen, I don't handle money.

Mr Berry What happened, Hazel?

Hazel (*innocent*) 'When I was a child I spake as a child, I understood as a child, I thought as a child: But when I became a man, I put away childish things.'

Hazel goes.
Mr Berry follows and stands in the open doorway.
Sound of speeding car offstage.

Mr Berry Little Hazel . . . death's ambassador, though she did not know it.

He re-enters the room, fists clenched in impotent despair.

Ruins . . . ruins.

He slaps the book shut and throws it away (words are no longer a solace).
Mrs Berry's shadow appears behind the glass screen and paces.

It was a Valentine's Day when Cooper called me in and sat me down. Even before he spoke a word, I guessed what was coming . . . and felt the full impact of my deceit . . . my deceits . . . Her growth . . . they had removed what they could . . . but there was still the risk of it seeding, that was his word, seeding . . . I came home and Gladys was here waiting . . . She looked up and flinched. We rallied, little things, treats, a ride on the *Greenwich Belle* along the Thames, all the way to Hampton Court . . . I put a rocking chair in the greenhouse . . . She loved . . .

Over his speech Mrs Berry's ghost has entered. She is wearing the white nightgown and white nightcap as in the earlier scene.

Mrs Berry (*finishing his words*) I love the smell of the tomatoes, before they ripen.

Mr Berry More than the roses, Gladys?

Mrs Berry Their skins so thick and green and filled with life . . . it makes me think of the miracle of health and the inverse miracle of disease.

Mr Berry Don't, Gladys, don't.

Mrs Berry (*sudden*) I don't want to lose my marbles . . . how long have I, Jack? (*Frightened.*) How long before it spreads to my brain?

Mr Berry It won't. I won't let that happen . . . I'll be your . . . chevalier.

Mrs Berry (*with a lovely smile*) Yes, and the not-yet-ripe smell of the tomatoes will – (*as she searches*) permeate . . . Versailles.

'Unpack my heart with words.' Of all the things I'd gleaned from you, Jack, that has stayed with me the most . . . because, I wasn't sure what it meant. (*Lucid.*) Whether it meant getting nearer to the other person or further away from the other person, which is to say a you or a me.

Mr Berry (*reassuring*) It is you, it is me.

Mrs Berry (*sudden*) Unpack my heart and cut it open.

She goes. He watches her, then turns to the audience.

Mr Berry It was in the hospice that it happened . . . her withdrawal . . . withdrawing from me . . . wouldn't say a word . . . She could speak, she spoke to nurses. 'I need you, Gladys, to say something . . . a few words . . . to hold on to.' At the very end she turned her face to the wall . . . Was that love or punishment? (*Walks downstage.*) Is that love and punishment?

Mr Berry, unnerved, takes a few steps backwards until he is by the glass-panelled wall (his back to the wall). He speaks, apparently rationally, to offset the terrors.

Mr Berry I knew this man Wystan from the cricket club
. . . blue blazer . . . quite dapper . . . had a one-night
stand . . . never clapped eyes on the lady again . . . One
morning, eighteen years later, a grown figure ascends
their flight of stately steps in South Wimbledon . . . wife
Margaret opens the door . . . Grown girl says 'Can I see
my father, can I see my father?' Spitting image of him,
same jug-ears, sandy hair, freckles . . . Door slammed in
her face . . . 'Come you down here,' wife Margaret shouts.
He was in his den . . . a bit of a dreamer, Wystan . . .
Warfare from that very moment onwards. Unceasing
warfare. (*Quiet.*) I hear he went mad in the end.

*Glass greenhouse flooded with light, full of growing
plants, their leaves swaying lightly.*

*Footfalls start up offstage. Mr Berry stares straight
ahead, expressionless.*

Curtain.